Secrets

of

Tutoring

What's inside me

WHY?

What's the point of this book? Do you know how hard it is to find a job these days? I'm betting you do, or else you wouldn't be interested in buying this book. It's a rough world out there and the job opportunities aren't getting much better, especially for those of us trying to get our feet in the proverbial job market door. I mean shit, of course you could grab a job at the local coffee shop or grocery store, and that's all fine and good. Doesn't it feel like a bit of a waste though? I mean, you spend so much time studying for exams and tests, and for what? Think of all the late nights and all the stress that led you to this point. Think of all the tuition fees, textbooks, and study groups. Wouldn't it feel like a kick in the nuts if we realised the only reason we went through that temporary hell was because we were "supposed to"?

It all felt wrong to me. I felt cheated. I was told my whole life to go to school, get an education, work my ass off and then "you'll be all set". Maybe in some sweet cosmic dreamland, sure! As many of you now know, that's just not the reality we have to deal with. In fact it's not even close.

Take me for instance: after getting an overall average of about 80% (notice that that's not a genius score – I'm smart but definitely not the smartest by any stretch of your imagination) in my undergraduate degree and master's degree, the only "real" job offer I had was to work for the government, and they didn't even care which school my degree came from or from which program. It seemed sweet at the time but trust me when I say that 90% of government jobs are soul sucking nightmares that seep inside you and suck your life away, one day at a time, haunting your children, and your children's children for innumerable generations to come. Hooray fun! I'm not bitter at all I swear.

Like most misinformed humans I thought the government job was my only grown-up choice. So I'll be honest even though I'm embarrassed about it - I took that government job that I then kept for 5 years. Worst move ever. I wish I had a mentor or a family member who would push me to realize at least part of my potential, instead of just sitting behind a desk waiting for my retirement. If I hadn't landed that job I could have built up my company twice as fast, and I would have not wasted 5 years behind a desk.

No retirement package, not any amount, is worth spending your 30 best years behind a desk.

This book is about realising some potential, and earning yourself some freedom from the ol' soul-draining 9-5. It's about how to use your nerd powers to create demand in any market. It's about being diligent and organized and strong enough to earn income for yourself. Think of how good it would feel knowing that through your cunning tutoring techniques, you earn enough cash-money to pay your rent, buy your groceries, pay your debts/credit cards and even have enough scratch left over to take some vacations. You will have no one to thank but yourself. That, is what this book is about.

But I'm not a student and I haven't been in a long time: Hey, don't sweat it. You don't have to be a 20-something or in school. The only truly vital skill that you need to bring to the table is subject mastery. Are there one or more courses that are being taught in local high schools or universities that you feel you can dominate? Could you get to the point where you would score at least 85% on the final exam? If you can get 85% or higher on the exam, then you can use this book and *start earning income for yourself and your family* or whoever the fuck else you want to support. Except Steve. Steve has to earn his own money.

No boss, no set hours, and no rules of any kind other than the ones you set for yourself.

Fuck. Yes.

MY BEGINNING

The first time I helped someone with their math work I was in high school. I wasn't particularly talented at tutoring and I didn't have any sort of magical grasp over the material. I just knew it better than my buddy did. It didn't matter though, since my friend's mom paid me $25 an hour for math help. That was huge money for me, especially considering minimum wage in my area at that time was probably around $7.

When I got to university, I worked for the math and physics departments tutoring students for $12 an hour.

What a rip off. I stopped tutoring for a while until I got to grad school, where I picked it up again at $25 an hour.

After grad school I took my government job and temporarily stopped tutoring all together. When I needed some extra cash, I worked for one of the main tutoring companies in my area at $17 an hour. I thought this was half decent considering they were doing all the marketing for me. That is, of course, until I realized that they were charging almost $50 an hour. They were taking more than 60% of the fee for themselves. Are you kidding me? What's worse is that the high school students that were working for that company were taking home the same amount as me. I had a master's degree for Christ's sake.

I, and all the other tutors working for this company were paying this company 60% of our income because we were scared of learning how to market ourselves, and scared of being solely responsible for the client's satisfaction.

Let's take a minute and put things in perspective. One of the biggest tutoring companies in Ottawa (my hometown) was charging $50 an hour to have a high school student, with almost no experience, teach other high school students math. Exqueeze me?

I was feeling guilty charging $25 when I was in grad

school. Not anymore, bitches! This crazy concept of feeling "guilty" for charging a high rate will be covered later)

So what was my problem? Why did I feel like $30 was too much to charge? As we shall see, it was pure noobery.

After about 5 years of experimenting with different methods and wasted investments, I learned how to solve the basic problems of starting a micro tutoring business. I went from earning $17 an hour while working for someone else to now earning on average about $100 each hour. I was able to quit my government job that paid almost $60,000 per year because I was earning more working for myself as a private math tutor. I wasn't working more than 5 hours a day, and I had no boss. Not having a boss may not seem like a big deal to you now, but just wait until you're working for some jerk who thinks he knows more than you and wants to boss you around just because he can. If that doesn't motivate you I don't know what will.

I've wasted probably $5000 on advertising trying to figure this stuff out. I've also wasted about 5 years of my life working for someone else while trying to get this business up and running. This book has everything you need, apart from the actual subject mastery, for you to become completely self-sustained on tutoring income.

If I moved to a new city right now, where I had no pre-existing clients and no referrals, I would be able to pay rent at the end of the month simply from tutoring income. I could get approximately 3 students the first week, and then 5 every week after that. Because I'm smart and I run group sessions, I make around $60-80/hr in that first month and work only 25 hours bringing in approximately $1,500. That's enough to make rent and credit card payments etc. That's for only 25 hours of work in the whole month. Nice.

This is the story of how to do it for yourself.

GET THE STUDENTS

This book is split up into 3 main sections. These sections are the bread and butter of tutoring: Get the Students, Teach the Students, and Run the Business. You need to eventually master each one of these components or you'll fall flat. The good news: everything you need to know is right here in this book. This section, "Get the students", is going to teach you everything you need to know about getting students through marketing techniques that are free and available to anyone. As for most new tutors, this is perhaps the most stressful aspect that comes to mind when you think about starting your tutoring business.

Relax, because with a little hard work and the information in this section, I *guarantee* you'll get as many students as you want.

Marketing

Tutoring is a lucrative business by any means, especially when you contrast it to the amount of work you have to do and the amount of schooling you have to have completed. You can become a tutor out of high school if you want, and start earning $40/hr right away. Crazy, right?

Assuming you have all your subject matter down pat, how the hell are you going to get your students?

The important thing to remember with marketing is that even the most effective methods bring in less business than you hope. When you're starting off, you expect marketing strategies like a website to bring you 100 new clients a day and destroy galaxies with ease. I'll say it ain't so, cause it ain't.

Expect the most effective marketing strategies to bring in approximately 5 new students a month.

Now here's the nice part: If you stack two masterful marketing strategies, like craigslist ads and our targeted emails (details about this to come, don't worry) you'll realize the gains of both. Using the techniques I'm going to show you in this book, you can get as many students as you can handle. Trust me.

We're also going to take a second to think about what *type* of students we are looking for. I'm going to show you that all students are not created equal in terms of both your financial gain and your general happiness.

Something I want to point out now: the most lucrative and dependable students are typically high school students. There are a couple of reasons for this. The first is that the subject matter is really easy, and it's very rare that you'll be caught off guard. The second reason is that the semester for a high school student is about a month and a half longer than a university or college semester, which means you're making bank for 6 more weeks from that student. That being said, *feel free* to use the same techniques with university students, just be aware that you'll be doing more work for a smaller pay off (even though the university courses can be a lot of fun to teach).

A great tutoring company is only as good as its great students

Before we dive into the actual strategies, let's do some quick math. Imagine you made $40 an hour. How many hours would you need to work per week to completely sustain yourself? Well, if we work a normal work week of 40 hours we earn $1,600 each week, and that's $6,400 in the month. That's not half bad, but it's also *practically impossible.* There is no way you can work 8 hours a day tutoring. You'll burn out and die for sure, leaving your children to suffer, starve, and be sold to the Egyptian Elite. Total frowny face!

In the tutoring world, working 5 hours a day tutoring is a big day. Think about it – in a 9-5 job you get a few breaks, lunch, and you can usually dick around for a few moments here or there on your Facebook page looking at babes on your friend's cousin's roommate's page. I would never regularly schedule more than 5 hours. I make exceptions near exam periods, but I'll never work a standard work day of 8 hours on the regular. Let's work smart and hard, not just hard.

Ok so let's say we work 5 hours a day, 5 days a week, for 4 weeks per month. That's $40 x 5 x 5 x 4 or $4,000 each month. You know what, that's not half bad either. Keep in mind that's your *introductory rate, which does not even include group sessions.*

Nice.

Now it's time to learn how to get those students. We know what we want and how much, let's just figure out how to do it. I've tried just about everything. Since I'm such a nice guy (honestly I'm not), here's a complete list of the marketing strategies I've tried over the years. In no particular order:

1.   Ads on Google
2.   Ads on Facebook
3.   Ads on Kijiji (local classified site)
4.   Ads on all tutor list sites (there are about 15 in my area that I keep up to date)
5.   Ads on Craigslist (similar to Kijiji)
6.   I paid hot girls to hand out "math is sexy" business cards outside math classes at universities (yes, I seriously did)
7.   Posted all over social media
8.   Emailed teachers from high schools
9.   Called all the local high schools, and submitted

my resume with the school's student services office

10. Offered discounts to students if they got me referrals

11. Built a few different websites (current one is www.tallguytutoring.com)

12. Changed my business name (from Sheldon Stewart Tutoring to Tall Guy Tutoring)

13. Got testimonials from students and parents and plastered them on my website

14. Sold my body for referrals (just kidding. Seriously, don't do this.)

Some of these strategies worked, and some of them fell flat and wasted my money. You'll never guess which ones work well and which ones didn't. Hey wait - I have a great idea! Let's talk about every single one, and order them from worst to best so that you'll be able to become a master marketer, and you'll be able to *save tons of money* by learning from my mistakes. Good talk.

The ineffective marketing

Paying hot girls to give out "math is sexy" business cards seemed like a hilarious marketing strategy to me, and I thought for sure it would work. After all, sex sells. So I tried to find a way to incorporate it into my marketing. It didn't take. This is a great example of a marketing strategy that builds reputation, but doesn't earn you students quickly. People are *definitely going to talk about you,* and in this case that's a very good thing. If our goal however is to get students quickly, this strategy isn't going to line the coffers right away.

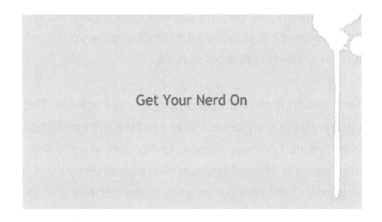

Get Your Nerd On

Ads on Facebook and social media are seen by a lot of folks but rarely convert into paying customers. If you need to pick up extra clients this is not going to do the trick. It will get your name out there, and people may start to think about you a little more, but I almost never got any students from Facebook advertising.

Offering discounts for referrals is essentially throwing your money away. If a student likes you, they'll refer you regardless. If they don't like you, they're not going to recommend you to a friend and risk tarnishing that relationship just for a discount on some tutoring. It doesn't work.

Also, I feel that discounts for referrals is something a company does to supplement lack of substance. Apple doesn't give out coupons (at least I haven't seen any) or referral bonuses because they know people love their products and they don't need extra incentives to buy. My advice is to not do it either, because you should have a similarly reputable service.

Testimonials did almost nothing for my business. This one really blew my brain. When I started out I thought that for sure I'm going to have to have some referrals from parents. How else would new clients know that I know my stuff? Well guess what. It doesn't matter at all.

When I did the analytics on my website, it shows how often people visit each different page on your webpage. This is a service that Google provides. In about a year, the testimonials page was visited only a handful of times. *Less than 10.* All the while I was getting more and more clients each week. It's far better to have a clean looking site then to have testimonials. People don't usually trust that shit anyway. I mean, read this,

"Sheldon was one of the most effective tutors we have ever had. Thanks so much Sheldon!" -Robert from Montreal

Sure there Robert. Sure there.

Do you believe that shit? No you don't and no one else does either. I made that shit up to fool you.

I'm not saying that referrals can't help your business

grow; I am saying that there are better things to spend your time on.

The medium effective marketing

The following strategies have actually gotten me some clients. So you should do them if you'd like to. The thing is, I don't do them anymore but that's because I'm not looking for new students, and when I am, I just double my efforts on the best marketing strategies. So consider these optional marketing strategies for the time being.

Google AdWords took me a while to learn, and it's a bit on the pricey side. It also requires you to stay up to date, at least slightly, with Search Engine Optimization (SEO) affairs. The reason for this is that it will cost you less when someone clicks on your ad if you use the right keywords and have your website built in an SEO friendly way.

Google
AdWords

Don't be intimidated by the learning curve of Adwords. It's a lot of fun to learn and since it's not your main way of marketing, you can take your time with it. So chill baby gurl.

That being said, I strongly suggest you do use AdWords, but only *after* you go through the best marketing strategies that I'm going to talk about. The reason is that you can use google AdWords for so many other things, not just your tutoring business. My knowledge in AdWords helped me sell this book, for instance. It's a powerful tool once you get to know it a bit. It just takes a long time to learn (about a month before you start to feel comfortable) so you'll want to get started now with the other marketing strategies, and do AdWords later. Move move move. Produce produce

produce. Fine tuning is done after you are up and rolling. Don't be a boob.

Ads on Kijiji, Craigslist etc. is a great way to get your name out there, but doesn't usually bring in the best clients. Remember that getting the *right* students is as important as any other aspect of running the business. Parents and students turn to Kijiji and other classified and local sites when they are in a panic. They don't, generally speaking, go there when they want a great professional tutor to help their child for the semester or term, which is ideally what you're looking for.

I would pay $500/student if I could upgrade them from unreliable and unmotivated to reliable, eager to learn & work

Think about if you were a parent of a child. Since the parent is usually the one who pays, they are usually the one who seeks out the tutor. Try and think where you would go if you knew you wanted to hire a tutor for the term. Would you take a risk on a person you have never met, don't know anything about, and whose ad you saw online? Or would you go to your school's student services centre where they have tutors that they've been referring to many of their students? It's an easy call (this is a hint for the best marketing strategies for tutoring...)

That being said, you can still get lucky and find great students on these sites. If you're going to go this route, I'm going to help you by giving you my exact template that I use when I post my classifieds ads. Here is my Apollo template.

Apollo Template

Ad title: Awesome Biology tutor (anything like this is fine)

Ad text: Hey there! My name is _____ and I love tutoring Biology 1001 (or whatever class name or subject like "math"). I also know why students struggle with the course, and love helping them finally understand.

I'm easy to get along with and I really love teaching!

I tutor on weekdays from 3pm until 9pm, and I generally like to meet at Main Street Library (put whenever and wherever you'd like to meet).

I'm looking forward to hearing from you, and to get started with this course!

Cheers,

Your Name

Nothing fancy, and it does the trick.

Having a great website is a really good idea and you should do it, but again only after you try what I show you in the next section. You actually don't need a website to be pulling in lots of clients. It does look professional, and will definitely help you in the long run though, so be sure to get this done. It's not urgent, but it's also not optional.

Don't make your website any more than **5 pages in total**. Make everything super simple, right to the point, and put a little personality in it. Check out www. tallguytutoring.com as an example. Websites with too much crap never perform well at all. My site probably has too much on it right now.

Look at how this shit pops. Aww yeah.

T.G.T. IS
THE BEST

Over 300 students taught and over 5,000 hours of tutoring completed

SHOW ME!

WE TEACH
ALL COURSES

All university math, especially from Ottawa U or Carleton. All elementary math, including reach ahead courses. All high school math or science. No problem.

WHAT WE TEACH

GET
REGISTERED

GET REGISTERED

Why are we the best?

At the end of the day there's only one thing that counts: value.

Professional help from a Masters Honours Graduate in Math. Affordable prices. Second to none experience with your exact course. It's awesome, and it's an easy call.

OK, I'M LISTENING

I made that site by buying a template on www.templatemonster.com for about $80. I then took 4 months to learn how to code websites. I would *never* do it that way again. Since we are only going to have about 5 total different pages on the website, (you can see my five pages at the top; Why us?, Courses, Register, Contact and the Home page) you can pay an html coder like $500 to do that for you and teach you how to make simple edits. You could even find someone on Craigslist or Kijiji.

I bought the pictures from www.shutterstock.com and there are tons of different sites where you can buy really great quality pictures. The picture on my homepage of the superman suit thing cost me $10, and I made the edits myself.

My logo is from www.TheLogoCompany.net and I paid $150 for it.

If I had to do it all again, I would probably make the website after tutoring for about 6 months so as to have a bit of extra money.

The best marketing strategies

There is an underlying method to all of this madness.

In this business, (and in many other service based industries) you need to learn the power of *reputation*. Think of all of these marketing strategies as different ways of building your reputation. The main goal isn't to get a shit ton of students, the main goal is to build an awesome reputation. Getting new students when you have an extremely good (or weird) reputation is no challenge at all. My reputation in my local area is strong enough that I no longer pay for ad space, and I **still** get lots of new students. Contrast that to when I started out, and was paying for Google AdWords, Facebook, Kijiji (you can pay to have your ad higher in the rankings) etc. for a total of around $500 each month.

Notice how I said good or weird reputation? Well, it's true for the most part. Think of it this way. Have you heard that MacDonald's food is not actually food? Of course you have, because if you're reading this you're probably human and live on earth. When humans hear something like "MacDonald's food is fucking gross and not even food", a lot of people think to themselves "you know what, I bet it's so gross. I should try it and see for myself how gross it really is". Boom. That's another sale made from "bad" or "weird" reputation.

If I am to carry the analogy over to tutoring, a "weird" reputation might be something like having a lot of tattoos, being a bit scary, assigning ridiculous amounts homework and having ridiculous expectations, etc.

Don't interpret having a bad reputation as something like not knowing your stuff, missing appointments etc. You can definitely take it too far and fuck yourself over. Don't do that.

"Give a man a reputation as an early riser and he can sleep 'til noon."
-Mark Twain

Emailing and calling the student services centre of each high school is a super effective method. This method, and the next, are going to be completely free. Oh my stars that's nice.

Each high school has one of these offices. They are there to help students make decisions about their courses, help them with social issues at school or to offer advice on where to seek outside help for their academics. Some schools call them guidance counsellors.

Emailing the office is fairly easy, but can be time consuming. First, get a list of all your local high schools from your yellow pages or Wikipedia (I used Wikipedia), and get the number for the school. Then, simply call the school at their main number, and ask to speak with student services office. Once they pass you through, you explain how you'd like to submit your information to be a tutor at the school. Most student services centres are extremely happy to have the help. They will usually ask for the following;

1. A list of courses you tutor
2. Your rates
3. Your contact information
4. Your resume or background in teaching
5. Occasionally they ask for a police check (get this done just in case. It's easy unless you have been getting into some trouble)

Since we are one step ahead, we're going to have all that stuff ready before we call. Here is a sample document that has everything together, except for the police check.

ShelHammer Template

Sheldon Stewart

(613) 668-2357

TallGuyTutoring@gmail

www.TallGuyTutoring.com

Hello parents, teachers and students! My name is Sheldon and I'm going to be offering tutoring in the UNIVERSITY STREAM GRADE 12 MATH COURSES listed below. I mean I'm sure you could twist my arm for other courses but these are definitely some pretty cool courses so I'll favour them over other ones.

I built this business because I LOVE teaching. But you don't go see a doctor because he loves practicing medicine, you see him because he knows his stuff. :D I have my Masters in Math from Waterloo and I've been tutoring these courses for 10 years. I know them very, very well. Most importantly: I can teach them very, very well.

MDM4U – Data Management	MHF4U – Advanced Functions	MCV4U – Calculus and Vectors
When do I use choose?! When do I permute?! Does order matter? Can I replace?! How many standard deviations am I away from the mean, and what does that have to do with the letter z? So many questions!! One simple answer; Go see the Tall Guy :D	Logs logs logs! How can you not love logs?!? Oh wait, I know! You're a teenager and you have a life. lol. But seriously I love these things and love teaching them.	Although I love a good derivative, my favourite part of this course is vectors. It's especially fun to teach as a lot of these concepts, especially geometrical proofs, are new to students.
Rates	**Availability**	**Location**
The most current rates are available at www.TallGuyTutoring.com	Mostly weeknights from 330pm until 830pm	All session held at (full address details available on the site)

Usually this will do the trick. Only sometimes will the representative ask for more details, like a resume. Have one ready in case they do, and be sure to keep it, tidy, short, and make sure it highlights how you will be able to accomplish your role as a tutor. In other words, make sure you highlight all your grades, tutoring experience, and courses that you have taken. Here's a sample of the content from mine. Be sure to include your own dates of graduation etc. and format it nicely. The following excerpt is just the content.

Sample Resume

EDUCATION:

M.Math, U Waterloo (High Honours)   January, 2010

B.Math, Carleton University (High Honours)   April, 2008

EXPERIENCE:

Tall Guy Tutoring   2008-present

Owner, Tutor

- Tutored math from the elementary level up to 3rd year university
- Prepared lessons for students
- Prepared test and exam review lessons
- More information at www.TallGuyTutoring.com

University of Waterloo Sept 2008 - Jan 2010

Teaching Assistant

- Taught tutorials to 1st year Calculus and Algebra students
- Graded assignments and answered questions in office hours
- Graded and proctored exams

ACTUARIAL EXAMS:

P – Passed July 26, 2011

FM – Passed October 20, 2011

INTERESTS:

- Piano; I have enjoyed playing for over 15 years
- Basketball; I played two years at Carleton, won two national championships
- Economics and politics; I write a blog on Mises.ca

Now that we're starting to contact a bunch of schools, we're going to need to keep track of which schools we have contacted. To do this, I suggest you use Google Sheets or Microsoft Excel. I use Google Sheets so I can access these files from anywhere. Make a quick list like below. I even put in a column regarding the list of grade 12 math teachers so that everything was in one place.

	School name						
fx							
	A	B	C	D	E	F	G
1	School name	Main Number	Website Address	Student services extension	First name	Last name	target eMails
2	Lisgar	613- 696	http://www.lisgar.ca/				F
3	Glebe	613- 2424	http://www.glebeci.ca/	x2199			b
4	Immaculata	613- 1	imh.ocsb.ca	option 2			Asked for police check resume in person - said weren't on the list
5	St. Patricks	613- 1	sph.ocsb.ca	option 2			ga
6	De La Salle	613-1	www.de-la-salle.cepeo.on.ca	x529 (incorrect extension 2014			
7	Hillcrest	613-1	http://www.hillcresths.ocdsb.	x233			h
8	Colonel By	613-	www.colonelby.com	x313			
9	Samuel Genest	613- 4	samuel-genest.ecolecatholiqu	x			
10	St Matthew	613-	mth.ocsb.ca	none			h
11	St. Petes	613- 77	peh.ocsb.ca	x231? extension went to secretary			t
12	Brookfield	613-1 0	www.brookfieldhs.ocdsb.ca	x520			@
13	Ridgemont	613-1	http://ridgemonths.ocdsb.ca/	x232			F
14	Gloucester	613-	https://sites.google.com/a/glo	x5090			P
15	Lester B Pearson	613- 3	lbh.ocsb.ca	x227			
16	Holy Trinity	613-6	trh.ocsb.ca				
17	St. Pius	613-2	pih.ocsb.ca	x231			

If you focus a solid week on getting organized and sending out all the emails and such, you'll start receiving clients from this strategy within the month. If you stay on top of things and continue to send out emails each new semester, you'll be rolling in the students within a year, but you'll have a steady client base within a couple of months.

Emailing individual teachers from local high schools has been one of my most effective marketing strategies ever. Teachers who care about their students want to have great tutors ready for any students that need extra help. Why not show some initiative and offer up your personable, professional services?

The reason this marketing strategy is so high on the

list is because if a parent gets a referral from a teacher, there's an extremely high chance that that tutor will score that student. Once you've established a good relationship with a teacher, that teacher could refer you students time and time again, at **no additional cost.** That's why I say the best strategies are free.

To start nursing your relationship with teachers, you'll need to get a list of email addresses of all the teachers in your subject area. What's a good way to do that? Luckily, we've already made the list of high schools. Use this to start calling the department heads of whatever your subject area is to find out who the teachers are. There is usually a math department, science department, etc. If you can't get specific teachers' emails, don't worry. The department heads will do just fine. Alternatively, if the school has a half decent website, you can get the list of teachers from there.

Tip: Always use "bcc" when emailing a group of people

Now that you have targeted the teachers and/or the department heads, you're going to want to draft an email for them. Here's a sample that I used for my math tutoring, and since this book is supposed to make your life WAY easier, I'm going to explain every single line so you can modify it in an hour or less to whatever course you're going to tutor. Shit yes.

Challenger Template

Hey folks,

"This email is for the Grade 12 Math teachers. I'm currently a tutor on your school's tutor list." — This line is relatively self-explanatory. I have it in my ad because I wanted to chat with only the grad 12 teachers. If you're not sure your email list of teachers has exactly the individuals you're interested in contacting, specify your audience here.

"I've been running www.TallGuyTutoring.com for a few years now and it's a ton of fun. Although I tutor every level in high school and up to 3rd year university (including stats, calculus, algebra etc.) I'm doing a bit of a switch to now only tutor grade 12 classes in high school in addition to the university courses. These courses are obviously way more fun to teach." — This paragraph is used to establish expertise while further identifying to the teachers the specific courses that I am interested in teaching. This is an optional paragraph.

That's why this email is only for the current and future grade 12 teachers of MCV4U, MHF4U, and MDM4U. — Here I list the exact courses

I'm interested in teaching. You can do the same.

Calculus and Vectors MCV4U

Although I love a good derivative, my favourite part of this course is vectors. It's especially fun to teach as a lot of these concepts, especially geometrical proofs, are new to students. – For each one of the courses I specified that I'd like to teach, I'm going to give a fun little description of the course to display expertise. Do this for each of the specific courses you'd like to tutor.

Advanced Functions MHF4U

Logs logs logs! How can you not love logs?!? Oh wait, I know! You're a teenager and you have a life. lol. But seriously I love these things and love teaching them. – Same as above

Data management MDM4U

When do I use choose?! When do I permute?! Does order matter? Can I replace?! How many standard deviations am I away from the mean, and what does that have to do with the letter z? So many questions!! One simple answer;

TallGuyTutoring.com. :D – Same as above

About me: I have two degrees in Math. I have an honours degree from Carleton University and I have my Master's degree in Math from Waterloo. I played a ton of sports. I play music. I've had a lot of troubled students with serious learning disabilities and I've helped students doing work at least 2 grades above their level. So it's a good mix of both. – list your qualifications here. If you don't have any degrees it really doesn't matter, especially once you have a solid reputation. Worst case scenario you just say something like "I achieved a 90% grade in this course and love teaching it", assuming you don't have a degree. It's so incredibly rare that someone asks me about my degrees.

My prices are on the site, and are currently $60 per hour. They may increase without notice but existing students never see a price increase. – It's good to list prices. Do that here, or specify what type of sessions you run, like maybe group sessions or whatever.

Students and parents can contact me at this email (tallguytutoring@gmail.com) or simply use my site. Both go directly to me. – You need to let people know where they should contact you. Remember that this email might

get forwarded along, so a return email
is important. The rest is fairly self-
explanatory.

Cheers and best of luck with the rest of this
term!
Sheldon (aka the Tall Guy)

Get Mathin'!
(Put address here)
Cell - 613 668 2357
Facebook - www.Facebook.com/TallGuyTutoring
Web - www.TallGuyTutoring.com

Look at this from the teachers' perspective. If you're a teacher with a few struggling students who risk failing the course, this email will come as a breath of fresh air. It's professional, personable, and it does a good job of showing expertise and professionalism. In my opinion, this email really conveys that I'm confident and that I know my stuff. Problem solved.

Remember that I've personally tried all these strategies and I'm telling you which ones are the best. Stick with it, it'll work. Trust me.

Scheduling & Location

Discovering an effective way to schedule your clients can change your tutoring life from absolute chaos to blissful order. In this chapter we'll contrast busy unorganized schedules with structured recurring schedules. There are pros and cons to each. Then we'll cover location, and talk about places that are good for tutoring, and places that are not so good or appropriate.

Scheduling

Let's talk about two different tutors, Jake and Sam, who

used two different approaches to schedule their clients. For fun, let's suppose that these two tutors are brand new, and just starting out, like you. Then let's compare who did what and see which aspects of their respective plans actually make sense.

Let's start with Jake. Jake is afraid that he won't generate that much business, so Jake accepts clients and asks them which time they would most prefer. That's the way most tutors start out, and it's the way I started out. He then books them for that time slot, which is usually an hour long. He realizes that most students only book one session per week, so he calls them or emails them each week to see which time they would like.

This method makes a lot of sense at first glance, because it feels as though we are maximizing our time, and the number of clients we are taking in.

Enter Sam. Sam is a bit more of a cool cucumber and takes things a little less urgently. Sam feels good about his knowledge base and so he isn't stressed about getting enough students. He knows that if he keeps up his marketing strategies and works hard for the student, that he'll end up filling his schedule one way or another.

Sam decides that as a result, he is going to pick:

1. The amount of time he wants to tutor each day
2. The specific times that work well for him
3. Times that are back to back, so he doesn't have to be stuck waiting for students or have his day split between 2 large chunks of work

Now let's see what happens to each of our new tutors.

What happened to Jake?

Jake realized some quick gains. In fact, Jake took home more money than Sam did in the first few weeks. Because Jake took students at any time during the day, he had way more availability, which was nice for clients. On the flip side, Jake spent far more of his time waiting for students, because sometimes he booked clients with a half hour gap or more in between sessions.

Mon 10/6	Tue 10/7	Wed 10/8	Thu 10/9
		8 – 9 Random Student	
	11 – 12p Random Student		
		1p – 2p Random Student	
3p – 5p Random Student	4p – 5p Random Student		
			6p – 7p Random Student
7p – 8p Random Student			

As the months went on Jake started to realize he had a problem. Although he was really busy, and word was beginning to spread about his smooth tutoring skills, it became increasingly difficult to keep his best customers happy, as he rarely had the times they wanted.

This made things difficult for Jake to keep regular clients coming back, and it also made it difficult for Jake to retain clients. Remember, it's important that your clients are in the habit of visiting you. You need to make tutoring a part of their week. Just like soccer practice is on Monday nights, tutoring is on Tuesday night.

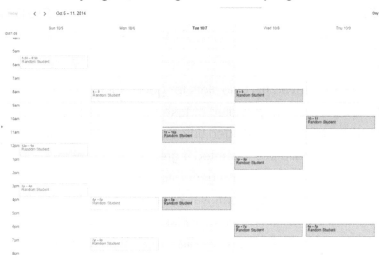

Even though Jake only had at most 3 students a day, most of his day was consumed with making trips to the tutoring location or waiting for students. No good.

What happened to Sam?

Sam started off business slow. Most of the customers
that were coming for help in the first month were
students who needed quick help or had a test the next
day. Sam didn't take these clients, as they were outside
his regular hours. This cost Sam some money, but he
slept well at night and wasn't stressed.

As Sam saved his time slots for good solid customers,
his calendar wasn't filled or taken up with crappy
customers who changed times or cancelled regularly.
When a solid client wanted a great weekday night spot,
Sam was available and generated steady income from
that client until the term was over.

As months went by, Sam built a reputation among the
various local high schools or universities. Sam was
able to keep all his appointments and was helping
students increase their grades and comprehension of
the material. This created a huge demand for Sam as
a reliable and effective tutor. As a result, Sam almost

completely filled his schedule and made some serious cash. All of that with no boss, and no rules. Nice.

Let's review some key components thus far. If you want to build your tutoring business into something that is steady and that you can depend on, you're going to need steady and dependable schedules, with steady and dependable clients. Unless you have enough money to have a secretary book all your sessions for you and you don't care about wasting two hours waiting for students each day, the only way to go is with a reliable and repeatable schedule. Without something that is repeatable from week to week, you won't be able to build tutoring as a habit for your clients, and you'll kiss your hard earned retention goodbye. Get used to doing the following things;

1. Build a habit - book weekly times for students
2. Pick times that you know you can never miss, and that you believe the client will never miss

Even if a client has initially asked for a chaotic schedule

with different times each week, take the initiative and ask them if there is one time that works well for them every week. It's important that you have a regular schedule so you can plan the rest of your life, but it's also important that the client can do the same.

Location

Location is a big part of tutoring. Luckily you don't have to be rich and have a huge empty room in your house to become a tutor. I tutored for years out of libraries, coffee shops, and students' homes. You want to make sure that the client is comfortable, but you need to balance this with logistics. It's no good that the client is comfortable in their location if you have to rush like crazy from your previous session and miss 15 minutes of your upcoming session. Not good!

It also doesn't make sense to be in a place where you can't hear each other. I don't think I need to spend any more time on why this is important.

Make sure that the place you've picked also has enough space for you to work. You don't want to feel cluttered or cramped. In fact, you don't want to have to worry about any distractions while you're teaching or trying to learn.

Finally, you'll want to make sure that you're in a place that is private enough so that the student isn't shy or embarrassed to make mistakes.

The five key points for location are therefore

1. Comfort
2. Convenience
3. Quiet
4. Space
5. Privacy

Comfort Picking a location where the student is comfortable is fairly easy. Most places with a table and chair meet that criteria, especially if you are only studying and working together for about an hour. Do not pick that wobbly table in the corner, nor should you pick crappy seating options like a stool (unless it's extra swanky). Get a sturdy table and a solid chair, or find a space that provides both. Don't sit on a couch and slouch over the coffee table.

Convenience You need to find an area that is close to where you live. Now that I have some momentum with my business, I tutor out of my house. This is obviously the best place as I can create an atmosphere that is conducive to teaching. If you can't tutor out of your house, or you live in a remote area which is far away from prospective students, don't worry for a second.

You're going to find a library in a local university or something like that. Before you have your first session at your planned location, arrive 30 minutes early or more to scope out a great spot. Don't ever put yourself in a situation where you feel rushed, if you can avoid it.

If you're picking a spot that is far from your home, make sure that you can get all your clients to that location. Don't be running around like crazy trying to make a ton of appointments at different locations around the city. There should only be two trips in your day: the trip from your home to the location, and then the trip from the location back home.

Quiet Even if there is a great university location near your house that is close to students, it's not going to do you any good if it's loud as shit. You need to find a place that is relatively quiet that will facilitate easy communication. Same thing goes for coffee shops. Don't pick one that is super busy, and don't sit near the door either.

Space In general I would say you always need room for one more person than you have. For example, if you're teaching 2 students you should have enough room for 3 people at your table. This is crucial for having a few different textbooks around if need be. You'll want quick access if you need to double check a formula or concept.

Privacy You'll need enough privacy so that the student feels like they can make mistakes and not feel judged. This is a key component for tutoring. Learning is about making mistakes and so you have to create an environment in which that can occur comfortably. Being too close to other people who might be listening in can affect this delicate situation. So, if possible, pick a place that gives a bit of privacy.

Here's a list of places you'll want to check out. If you're tutoring out of someone's shop, like a local coffee shop, ask the owner first and buy a coffee every time you go. They should appreciate that you're bringing in new students and parents that will now know about the shop.

1. Coffee Shops
2. Libraries
3. Universities (you can even book a room sometimes, especially if you're a student)
4. Your living room or dining room table

Effective scheduling and picking a great location are going to go a long way in building your business and ensuring a stable, consistent flow of clients on which you can depend. Remember that if this is your source of income, you'll need steady cash flow for rent, food, etc. This is the best way to make that work with absolutely zero stress.

The real money & value

Eventually, you'll reach a point where you can't really charge more per hour for a one on one session. I'm at $80 per hour (recently increased from my $60/hr rate) now and I don't see that going too much higher in my area. I'm already 4 times higher than the average rate (but still have happy customers because of my reputation). That being said, I don't even like to do one on one sessions anymore because even $80 an hour isn't hitting my target rates.

If we're smart, which most of us are, we can still add value to clients and get more money at the same time.

This is accomplished by group tutoring. Let me explain how truly awesome this business practice is when it comes to tutoring science, math, or any discipline that requires the student to do exercises to learn the material (languages work well with this model as well).

Let's say I'm doing a standard one on one session with

an average student. More often than not, they are going to come in with a topic that they need to learn from class. So, either the student or I (usually it's me) will find a problem to work on. I'll briefly talk about the problem and then I'll say something like "OK, now you're up to bat. I'm going to give you 3 minutes to solve this problem any way you like".

This is a crucial step in tutoring. The student needs to get comfortable and confident with the fact that they, not you, will be doing all the work. I also make a point to say that they can do it "any way they like" so that hopefully they don't depend as much on lists or formulas to solve it.

Here's my point - when a student is working away at the problem, you are doing nothing. You talk for maybe 2 minutes, and then they work for 5 minutes. Usually, this process repeats for the duration of the session.

This means you could have more than one student at the same time, with *no loss of value* for the student, and you just doubled your hourly income. Sweet.

Here are some other options for group tutoring.

1. 5 students come for the same 2 hour block
2. 2 students come for the same hour block
3. If students are all from the same class, you could

do 10 students in 2 hours

4. Run an exam review class at a university, and get up to 50 students for a 3 hour review

Obviously you can be creative here and find group solutions that work well for you.

Get it done

Instead of just seeing that list of options for group tutoring and saying "OK, that makes a lot of sense but requires a lot of organization", let's actually get some work done.

Right now, take a few minutes to think up a group solution that you are comfortable with. If you're just starting out, maybe pick something easy like "2 students in one hour". Either move two of your existing students into the same time block, or wait until you get two new students by doing some more sweet marketing. If you're charging $40 for each student, you'll make $80 in that *one hour alone*.

Once you've done it once, it's time to repeat the process. Try and get two group sessions set for every week. Make that your next goal.

Once you get to 3 or 4 students, you could charge $60 for two hours. You could do this until you have about 5 students coming in the two hour block.

In one of my two hour blocks I'm making $300, as I have 5 students paying $60 each. I only really work those two hours each day. Isn't that crazy? Sometimes it pays to be smart. Now I can use the rest of my day to find another dope way to make money, or just tutor more and earn even more money. Not bad for being self-employed.

TEACH THE STUDENTS

This is obviously the most important part of being a tutor. If you can't teach the students, then it doesn't matter if you have the best policies or location. If you can't teach well, you got nothin'!

So how do you teach well? How do students learn? In short, it's a combination of subject mastery and patience. There are a ton of resources out there on teaching but in my 15 years of teaching experience, I'm going to show you the concepts that stick out the most.

Students learn by forming patterns and connections in their own brains. They need to see and understand the pattern before they convert it into knowledge. So our job is to make the pattern accessible so that they can recognize it, and convert it. A subtle, but vital conclusion that can be drawn is that *the student has to want to learn.* If the student doesn't want to learn, you can't form the connections in their brain for them.

Our job is to make the pattern accessible so that the student can recognize it

That's your job. Sounds easy. It kind of is, once you get the hang of it and once you master your material. You have to realize that it's *the student* who learns the material. You *can't learn it for them.* It's a subtle distinction that you'll need to learn to be maximally effective. Obviously you'll be teaching them but the learning really happens on their end. It's the difference between "I've taught it to them so they understand" and "I've taught it to them but I'm not sure they get it yet, I'll have to do some more examples with them until they demonstrate to me that they understand the concept."

The second rule of thumb to keep in mind is this: help the student learn to completely detach from right and wrong. You want to do your best to encourage the student to not worry about getting a question wrong, and not worry about getting a question right. Instead, focus on what the student thinks is true. I repeat: do not focus on whether an answer is right or wrong. Instead, focus on what the student thinks is true. This is equivalent to saying that the student needs to fully understand a problem, not just know how to solve it.

Working through a problem

Here is the general flow of how I work through a question with a student. Of course there are exceptions, but tutoring sessions are filled with more of these types of scenarios than any other.

Task: Find a specific problem

The first thing you'll notice is that it's 100 times easier to handle a specific question than a general concept. If a student asks you to explain "equations", don't start rambling on about equations. It's too general, and you probably won't answer their question. Instead, ask them what they'd like to know about equations, or to see one of the problems from their homework about the topic.

I've lost many students over the years. Not only have I lost them, but I've had students come for the first trial session (which is still always a paid session) and then never come back, even though they indicated they were looking for a tutor for the semester. I would say at least 90% of these students came in with general questions. I did my best to answer them, but alas, the students left unsatisfied and kept saying "that's not what my teacher said".

How was I supposed to know that their teacher used a different method? It doesn't matter. Just get a specific question and don't answer general inquiries.

Task: Let them try the problem
Now that we have a specific question to work on, I might start by saying something like

Me: "OK let's have a look at this problem"
Student: "Sure, sounds good."

Oddly enough, I do almost nothing now. I just sit and wait for the student to read through the question and start working. If I am working with a group of students, I'll now move on to the next student and give the original student a bit of time to work through a problem. If they do nothing I might come in after a minute or two and say "How's it going?" If they know what to do, let them finish the problem and move onto a harder one, or a new concept. If they are a little bit unsure, they'll say something like "Is my answer correct?" or "I feel like I made a mistake" or "I think that's right". This leads nicely into our next task.

Task: Teach them to lose the attachment from right and wrong: At this point you should realize that the student still has a big attachment to right and wrong. You want to bring the focus back to *understanding*. Check out how a good tutor and bad tutor would handle the student's question of "is my answer correct?"

Bad tutor says "yes" or "no"

Good tutor says "do you think it is?" or "I have no idea (jokingly). What do you think?" or "I could tell you but I'd have to kill you (depending on age appropriateness of course). You don't know for sure?" or "How can we know for sure" or "convince me" or "why would it be?"

We teach confidence as much as we teach subject matter

Now, suppose that the student is a bit lost and needs some subject matter help. This isn't a confidence issue, they just have no idea what to do next. OK, great. This is where you can really use your subject mastery and break things down.

Task: Break things down. All the way.

Did you know that trigonometry is just a naming convention for the various ways to divide side lengths from a right angled triangle (this is a triangle with a 90 degree angle)? Trigonometry is a simple concept, built up to be difficult as the implications of trig are far reaching and vast. But the fundamental principles of trigonometry are elementary. I mean literally, I can teach trigonometry to a 6th grader. They of course won't have the algebraic tools to solve the same problems as a student in high school, but I can teach them the concepts of SOH CAH TOA in an hour or two.

In fact, the vast majority of the concepts from high school math and science share this property. They are all actually quite basic when you completely break them down. I bet I could teach anyone reading this book basic trig, right now. If you're smart enough to read, you're smart enough to understand this. It'll also be a good explanation of how to fully break down a concept.

Trig is just a naming convention for the different ways you can divide side lengths in a right angled triangle. We'll come back to this over and over. Might as well get it sunk in that nice brain of yours now. It's just a naming convention. Trig is more of a language skill than a math skill. Weird right? Let's check it out.

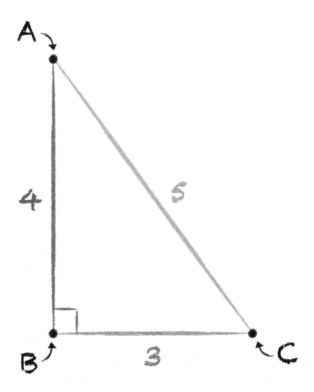

There are three "corners" to every triangle. In this case they are labelled A, B, and C. There are three sides to every triangle. In this case, we've got a side length connecting A to B (RED), a side length connecting B to C (BLUE), and one from A to C (GREEN).

If you wanted to, you could measure each side length. So let's do that. Let's suppose that RED = 4cm, BLUE = 3cm, and GREEN = 5cm.

Now let's say I wanted to talk about the numerical

result of dividing the length of the RED side by the length of the GREEN side. In this case, it's really easy, because we have a nice diagram with coloured sides and everyone is happy. We would just write down 4/5, because the red side is 4cm and the blue side is 5cm.

A super nerdy person might ask, how many ways can I divide all of the sides? For example, I could do RED/BLUE which is 4cm/3cm, or I could do BLUE/GREEN which would be 3cm/5cm, etc.

Let's consider *all* the different ways we can divide the different side lengths. We can do six different divisions, like this;

1. 4/5 (RED/GREEN)
2. 3/5 (BLUE/GREEN)
3. 4/3 (RED/BLUE)
4. 5/4 (GREEN/RED)
5. 5/3 (GREEN/BLUE)
6. 3/4 (BLUE/RED)

The problem now is that there are 6 different fractions (also called ratios), and it's hard to say which one I'm talking about at any given time - hence why trig is a language problem. To solve this problem, mathematicians came up with the naming convention of "sine", "cosine" and "tangent", which when used properly, can identify which ratio you're talking about at any given time. They are weird titles but they do the trick.

There are other weird trig names like "cosecant", "secant" and "cotangent" but we won't get into those. We'll just talk about basic trig which is sine, cosine and tangent. With those basic trig names, we are only able to identify ratios 1, 2, 3, and 6.

To identify one of the four fractions, use the following table which describes the naming conventions.

	Sine	Cosine	Tangent
Purpose	The purpose of all of these "trig ratios" (Sine, Cosine and Tangent are called "trig ratios") is to help identify, when given a right angled triangle, which of the six possible fractions you'd like to talk about		
Procedure	Each trig ratio must be "paired up" with a corner. You could never say just "sine" or just "tangent". You would have to say "sine & corner A" or "tangent & corner C"		
Choosing the corner	None of the trig ratios work particularly well when you choose the corner with the right angle, in this case corner B is the flop. You can choose from any of the other two corners, which are thought of as representatives of the angle inside the triangle at that corner.		
Possible ratios that can be identified	Sine and Cosine always identify ratios that divide by the longest side. So from our list, that leaves only fractions 1 & 2, which are 4/5 and 3/5 respectively.		Tangent always identifies a division of the two shorter sides. It doesn't ever deal with the diagonal side of a right triangle. In this case tangent can only identify ratios 3 or 6, so 4/3 or 3/4 respectively

	Sine	Cosine	Tangent
What to do when the corner is chosen	Of the two available short sides, sine identifies the short side which does not touch its chosen corner, and then divides it by the diagonal (which is also the longest) side.	Of the two available short sides, cosine identifies the side that is touching the chosen corner, and then divides it by the longest side in the triangle.	Of the two short sides, tangent identifies the short side that is not touching its chosen corner, and then divides it by the remaining short side.
What happens if we choose corner A?	Since sine takes the side that is not touching its corner and divides it by the diagonal side, "sine & corner A" = 3/5	Since cosine takes the side that is touching its chosen corner and divides it by the diagonal side, "cosine & corner A" = 4/5	Since tangent chooses the short side not touching its corner and divides it by the other short side, "tangent & corner A" = 3/4
What happens if we choose corner C?	Since sine takes the side that is not touching its corner and divides it by the diagonal side, "sine & corner C" = 4/5	Since cosine takes the side that is touching its chosen corner and divides it by the diagonal side, "cosine & corner C" = 3/5	Since tangent chooses the short side not touching its corner and divides it by the other short side, "tangent & corner A" = 4/3

"If you can't explain it simply, you don't understand it well enough." - Albert Einstein

This quote applies to calculus, basic math, physics, computer science, abstract algebra or anything. Learn your material really really well.

Task: Forget the formulas and the step-by-step

If you understand your subject and have mastery over it, formulas and rules and step by step processes, which are usually a student's "best friend", become the enemy and are usually just in the way. In fact, it's precisely because of this eventually huge list of formulas and step-by-step processes that students hate math and science. They see 100 formulas and think "How am I ever going to remember all of these?" or "How am I ever going to remember all these steps?" They're right, they usually can't and neither can I. Not unless we understand the concepts.

Caution: At first glance there may seem to be some exceptions. Sometimes the explanation of why something is true seems to be just so much work that it's not worth the pay off, and it doesn't really connect to other concepts. The "quadratic formula" is a good example. Students don't seem to necessarily need to know why that works. They do, however, need to know why it's used, how to use it, how it translates onto a graph etc. I would caution you to learn about these topics because often they are not very hard to understand, and it makes remembering them a hundred times easier. For example, quadratic formula is simply completing the square on a parabola in standard form $(ax^2+bx+c=0)$

Task: Prodding to see if the student understands

It's not always logistically reasonable to give a student problems on a related topic to see if they understand. Occasionally, you have to explain something quickly and just move on to the next topic. When this happens, it's a good idea to do a verbal check to see if the students understand. However, proceed with caution.

Don't simply ask "Do you understand?" Why not? Think about it. Let's say you're talking with someone you respect and want to impress. If they ask you if you understand a concept, you're probably going to say yes. It's easier to say yes and appear smart than to say no in that situation and require everything to stop just for you. So, you're going to have to be a bit sneaky when probing for information from your student. Try one of these;

1. Is there part of that that I can explain differently?
2. OK, was that confusing?
3. That's a bit tricky, isn't it?
4. Would you like to do some practice problems on this?

What do you notice about all of these questions? Here's what I notice: if you answer "yes" to any of these, it'll force us to work more on the concept. You have to go against your natural habit and say "no" to me if you want to move on, which means you probably understand the topic.

Task: Teaching confidence

A lot of the time students actually know how to do a problem, but they are so scared of getting it wrong that they say "I don't know". If this is the case, reply back "yes you do", and just wait. Encourage them and lead them to be confident.

There is a fine line between helping the student too much (essentially doing their work for them) and not helping enough. When you find that sweet spot of helping just the right amount, confidence is going to grow.

In fact, you can even go a step further when you're teaching confidence. When a student says "I know this question", and they prove it by getting it right, *challenge them.* Ask them, "Oh yeah, how do you know for sure?" or "couldn't it be this?" and offer an alternate solution that is incorrect. Alternatively, offer them a twist in the question that makes it much harder. "OK, how about this?" This process of continually challenging the student and having them succeed will build their confidence. Keep pressing, and keep expecting a lot of your students. They are all capable and you must lead them to realize this. Hey, it's your job. It is infinitely more important to teach confidence than to teach math or science or whatever your subject matter is.

It's not ever a bad idea to post in big writing on your wall:

Stop trying to get questions right. Start trying to understand.

Let's summarize what we've covered so far.

1. Be specific. Suggest a problem to the student or talk about a question that they bring to you. Don't talk about general crap.
2. The students have to try the problem first. Don't jump right in and solve it.

3. Help them lose the attachment to right and wrong
4. Break down concepts all the way. Get mastery of your subject as much as possible.
5. We teach students how to learn and how to be confident. Don't give up on this and just answer all their questions straight away.
6. Make sure the students understand. Either assign questions and have them explain them to you, or if you can only do a verbal check, make sure to use the right language.
7. Teach confidence. Have faith in their ability to learn. Build them up with small manageable steps until they are doing really challenging stuff.

Different styles: Coaching vs. answering questions

About half my sessions with students involve the student asking me question after question. These are the easier sessions to orchestrate because as long as you know your stuff, and you follow the basic teaching rules we set up earlier, the session will go by super-fast and the student will learn a lot. These sessions orchestrate themselves. You'll seem like an orchestration wizard. Nice.

The other half of the time you have students that are coming to learn from a mentor, not just a tutor. They won't really have things to work on other than general things like "geometry" or "mechanics". If this is the case, take the lead. Find something specific and suggest that you work on that together. Check out the resources section to find a whole bunch of good places to have ready during your sessions when this happens.

Teaching students how to make mistakes

If the student can't comfortably make mistakes, their learning is going to be severely limited. So why not have a few strategies in your back pocket to help them learn that mistakes are part of the game?

If you're noticing that your student is having a really hard time making mistakes, and it's preventing their learning, try this awesome trick:

Switch roles with the student. Let them know that they're going to be teaching you the material, and to get started, they need to explain to you what they know about the subject. Have them write it down if it helps, and it usually does. Do this for a specific question from their textbook. Have them take you through step by step how to solve it.

Caution: Don't discuss this strategy with the student, just go ahead and do it. Just say something like "ok can you explain this part to me? What do you know about this question?"

Not only is this going to help the student find the missing parts in their understanding, but it will illuminate to you where their gaps are. Help them along as they try and describe you the problem if they're making mistakes.

This method will also build their confidence a little bit. Confident students like making mistakes more than non-confident students.

As soon as they make a mistake in their explanation, ask "why is this part true?" Don't just say "no that's wrong". Don't ever focus on the fact that a solution is right or wrong. Focus on *why* a solution is right or wrong.

In fact, even if they write down the correct answer but you are unsure if they are 100% positive, be sure to test them on it. Ask "why is this part true?" If they get it right, it's going to build their confidence even more.

Students need to learn confidence in their work. That's one of the main things we teach; *confidence.* How do you teach that? You teach it by not being a crutch for the student to depend on every time they need help, but rather in key select times. If they need help with the concepts, help them in the way we described above. Give them only enough so that they can now form the connections and patterns in their brain, and then test them. If they just need comfort, don't help them. They can do it. Let them know that they can do it. You teach them how to help themselves, and how to get a question right without you helping in the least. Now that's confidence.

As they start to get easy questions correct and move into more complex questions, their confidence is really going to grow.

Resources

This section is going to help you be prepared for your sessions. It's going to tell you everything you're going to need to run a smooth session.

Depending on the courses that you like to tutor, you're going to need to build a list of good sites for information, collect good textbooks etc.

If a student comes in and has a bunch of questions regarding their own material, you might not need that many good resources, unless they are asking about something that you are unfamiliar with. However, if the student is coming to you and you are expected to have problems for them and to lead the session, you're going to need a solid list of resources.

The key to a solid resource collection is to build it slowly over time. Don't go crazy all at once and spend $5,000, as you might end up buying the wrong things. In fact you don't need to spend any money if you don't want to. Just use the internet. Gotta love those sweet sweet interwebs.

Building your online resource database

Obviously there are a lot of resources online. Like, tons. The goal isn't going to be necessarily to find the best ones, but rather to find really good ones that do a great job. Then, once you've found them, keep them organized. Every time you find a better site, replace your old crappy one. Easy peasy. This way you don't have to stress about finding the ultimate combination of sites before you start tutoring.

Here's how I suggest you keep your bookmark bar organized.

1. Make a folder for each class you teach
2. If you ever use a site during your sessions, add it to that folder. Feel free to add the same site to multiple folders.

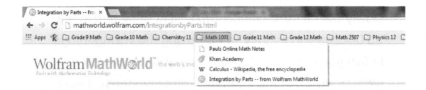

Now, every time you tutor that course, you don't have to fish around for all the good sites you use. You'll have it ready to go in a split second. That's going to come off very professional. Nice job.

Textbooks

I have a nice collection of textbooks that I use. I fish around on used sites all the time looking to pick up textbooks that students are frequently using.

If you're going to go this route, I definitely suggest you fish around on all your local used sites like Craigslist before you buy a new book. Textbooks are great to have around to assign problems to students. The internet does a shitty job of this, generally. Textbooks are chock-full of examples.

They also usually have the exact material the students are covering. Ever been on Wikipedia looking for something specific about, say, trigonometry, and you get "history" and "applications" etc.? Who cares about that shit?!? I want to know how to "insert exact topic here". Textbooks are better than internet for that, too.

Short list of sites that I regularly use

1. Khan academy (for pretty much all courses)
2. Desmos.com (best free online graphing calculator)
3. Paul's online math notes
4. Wolfram Alpha (great for integration problems)
5. Wikipedia

Nerves

When I started off tutoring this was by far the biggest hurdle. I was really concerned with the thought that, "Holy shit, if I'm charging people money for tutoring, I better know all their material perfectly, and I better be able to answer their questions on the spot! Otherwise, they're definitely going to call me a fraud, not pay me, and I'm going to be super embarrassed!" The good news is that this isn't true in the slightest. In fact, I still get questions today that I don't quite know the answer to. So don't worry, if you're having problems with nerves, we're going to handle that in this chapter.

When I tutor now, my nervousness levels are between 0% and 3%. I'm a bit nervous for new clients, but after I've met them and know where they're at, I completely lose all my worries.

Here's a summary of the things we're going to talk about in this chapter:

1. How to handle questions that you don't know the answer to.
2. What not to say when you don't know the answer.
3. How to reduce nerves, even if you do know the answer.

Remember, you are the expert. The student hired you because they perceived you to know what you're talking about. *You're the expert*. This means that you should definitely not worry about trying to "prove yourself". Don't show off about stuff that you know in the class, and don't stress about having to know every single thing.

Even if you go talk to a lawyer or an accountant, they still occasionally have to check up on a fact or make mistakes. When they do they'll then simply fix the error and move on. So we'll do the same.

How to handle questions you don't know the answer to

Honestly it's no biggy. This happens to me a lot and I just say "hmm. I honestly have no idea". lol. That's the easy part. But now we have to learn about and solve this problem ASAP.

As soon as I realize I don't know the answer, I go searching for it. I would say take no more than 3 minutes to track down information on the question. Where do I look? Here's my top list, in order

1. Their notes from class
2. Google and my saved sites
3. My textbooks on the subject
4. My notes that I've compiled from previous years

Always go to their notes first. Sometimes their teacher taught a concept with a slight little twist, and it threw me off. The problem is that if I go online right away, I might not find that specific twist. So, notes first. Always.

If I haven't made any headway at all in 3 minutes, I call it quits and say "Ok I'm going to have to get back to you on that one. I really have no idea".

If I have made significant headway into the problem, then I decide whether I keep going or call it quits anyway. I don't want to waste too much of their time.

What not to say when you don't know the answer

One thing we are going to learn to never do is to fake our way through a problem. Never pretend you know something that you don't. Faking it is the best way to make sure that the client doesn't come back for more sessions. If you really don't know how to do a problem and you know for sure it would take you more than 3 minutes to find out, forget about it and say "yeah I have no idea. I'm going to have to get back to you".

Imagine you're in the doctor's office, and you're feeling really sick. You say to the doctor, "what's up Doc, I feel sick and I want to know why!" Let's suppose that he honestly has no idea whatsoever. Would you prefer him saying "Well you see, sicknesses can take on a variety of forms, blah blah blah" or would you just rather "I'm not sure right now. We're going to have to do some more tests."

One of these answers is professional and gets straight to the point. The other one is vague and will make you doubt your doctor. You can easily tell when someone is faking it like that, because *he can't offer a solution.*

How to reduce nerves

Here's a few techniques I use to reduce nerves. It's actually kind of the same technique I use for going down on a scary roller coaster or down a big water slide. I say to myself "this is happening, let's figure out how best to deal with it".

1. Accept that you're going to do it.
Don't toy around with cancelling a session because you're nervous. Accept that the student is coming to

meet you, and that you're going to be doing your best and the rest is out of your control.

2. Realize that how much or even if they like you is mostly out of your control.

If you've done all your prep and know the material, there isn't a whole lot else that you can do.

3. Geniuses don't usually come for tutoring.

All the kids and adults who come to tutoring are smart. You need to believe that and they need to believe that. On the other hand, they probably aren't coming to get help because they have a 99% in the class and need help with that extra 1%. Chances are good that they are closer to the 50% mark, and that you're more than qualified to help them out.

RUN THE BUSINESS

Now that we have tips on how to get students and how to teach them, we have to remember that there is still a business to run. I've been tweaking the pricing, bookkeeping, and client policies for years and have come to some interesting conclusions. Luckily for you, you'll get them all.

Pricing & Bookkeeping

This is an important topic because it's going to set the stage for what type of tutoring business you are going to run. I strongly advise you charge far more than what the other local tutors are charging. Charging a competitive rate makes it seem like you are offering the same product as the other tutors, *but you're not.* You are armed with the tools in this book so you know the ins and outs of the business and you know exactly what to do to earn the higher pay.

I just looked on my local site for tutors and most tutors are charging $20-$30 an hour. Nice try guys. I charge $80 per hour, and my group sessions earn me even more (but clients pay less).

Why do parents and students want to go with me when it costs them 4 times as much? Because I've been referred by other students and teachers, and they know I'm a professional. They are paying a higher price to relieve themselves the stress of worrying that their tutor might be shit. People pay to feel better and to have less stress.

Set your price high, and wait for the clients to come.

I've had prospective students yell at me (through text) for having such high prices. "That's outrageous" is very common. You know what else is common now? Earning really great money week after week. Students who complain about the high price are not the clientele you seek. They want cheap tutoring and they will no doubt have extremely high, frequently unreasonable demands.

I would start my rate at double the rate of whatever the average price is for tutors in my area. Then as I become more and more busy, I'll up the fees.

Setting a high price is very nerve racking. I know this from experience. Don't worry about it, just work really hard at making sure your client is happy. After having many happy clients at your rate, you'll start to feel better about it. Then you just have to enjoy the sweet sweet money rolling in :) Everybody wins. Putting some positive stress on yourself is never a bad thing.

Bookkeeping

One of the interesting things about this business is that I've never ever had a student not pay. I've had to chase down money a few times, but they always pay in the end.

It can be a bit of a challenge to keep track of who has paid, and who hasn't. Sometimes people pay for only one session, but sometimes people pay for the whole month. Trust me, it can get confusing. If you mess up and accidentally ask for payment from a client who has already paid, you'll look really silly. Also, you don't want to forget to ask for payment. That sucks even more.

So we need a good system to keep track of everything. Here is the template that I use. If you don't know how to use excel, you should. It's easy so just learn the basics and be done with it.

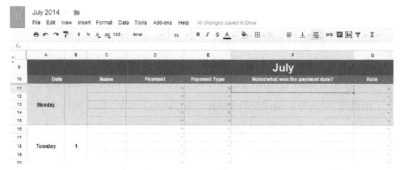

Policies

Because there are so many different types of students and parents out there, you're going to want to protect yourself with some policies. You're going to want a policy that covers payments, cancellations, and any other situation that has a potential to create conflict. If you get all these topics covered in a nice policy, you can just add it as a block signature at the bottom of all your emails so that clients have access to it when they need it. Done and done!

In this section we'll go through my current policy that is attached to the signature block of every one of my tutoring emails. This way you can see the general look and feel that I like to use. Feel free to tailor it to reflect your own personality. After all, a fun a cool personality is part of why students will come to you.

Payments

How I'm getting paid

There are a ton of different options regarding how you're going to be paid. Let's go through some of the options and see why I like them or don't like them. You'll have to decide what you'd like to do, then add that to the 'payment' section of your policy.

1. **Cash:** This is by far my favourite method of getting paid. It's quick, effective and also it gives

me cash so I don't have to go to the ATM all the time!

2. **Email money transfer:** This is another great way to be paid. You have the money in your bank right away and also you have a record of the payment, so you can always check and see who paid how much and when.

3. **Cheque:** A lot of banks now offer cheque deposit through your mobile phone. This is a sweet option, but you have to do a bit more organization. Keep an envelope each month with all your cheques from that month. The system for depositing cheques is still working out some kinks, so be sure to keep all the cheques. Cheques are also nice because if there is ever question as to how much someone paid, you have the record in hand.

4. **Credit Card:** Setting this up isn't hard, but I also don't like this option. The credit card company takes a cut of your hard earned money. It also doesn't really provide added convenience. Why do I say that? In all my years of tutoring, I have not **ONCE** been asked if I accept credit cards. For some reason, parents and students just don't think to pay for this particular service with a credit card.

When I'm getting paid

In all my years of tutoring I have never, **EVER** not been paid for a session. There have definitely been a few instances where I was worried that I wouldn't be paid, but good human nature has prevailed in each case. So stop worrying about *if* they're going to pay and start worrying about *when*.

There are a few different payment plans you can choose. Let's go through them so you can decide which ones work for you. You'll be able to see the ones I use later.

1. **Pay on a per session basis**: This would mean that the student or parent brings the payment to each session, and only pays for that session. This method is really the only option for students who are coming to see you for that test tomorrow, and that`s fine. You don't want to use this method for your regulars, though. That'll be covered in the client retention section.

2. **Pay for the whole month:** This is the method I use for about 90% of my clients. After a trial session to make sure it's a good fit, I ask for payments for the month. I just say "I ask for payments for the month" when they ask about money. This gives you an extra layer of

protection in case a student cancels on you last minute. You're the one with the cash. Nice. I also ask for the month's payment before the start of each month. If they pay me for the following month on our last session of the previous month, that works best.

3. **Retainer:** A retainer is a bunch of money that the student gives you (like $500) that they just use up as you tutor them. This method works fine and actually gives them the incentive to use all that money up. I don't use this method generally but have considered using it more regularly. You might want to give it a try and see how it goes.

4. **Postdated checks:** My old piano teacher used to do this. She would ask for postdated checks for the *whole year.* Tutoring can't work the same way as most of the time the students are only studying for 4 months. Once you build yourself a small reputation, you can easily ask for postdated checks for the remainder of the term. If you do, it'll mean you definitely should never cancel on them. I like to have a bit more freedom to take a vacation or two each year so I don't really use this option.

When you write out your policy, just pick your favourite

way of getting paid. Don't list 800 different ways to do things. List just one, and the client will let you know if they have a problem with that.

Here's the part from my policy that addresses payment options:

Payment time: I ask for payment for the month at or before the first session of the month (if you are not on a weekly schedule with me, please send payment to each session or send via email shortly after the session.)

Payment type: I ask for cash, but accept email money transfers as my second choice and cheques (made out to Sheldon Stewart as opposed to Tall Guy Tutoring) as my last preference.

Cancellations

Cancellations are the bane of a tutor's existence. The perception is that we're younger than most professionals, and therefore less professional. This becomes problematic in instances where a student doesn't really feel like coming to a session (or they want to miss a session for some other reason), and the parents feel they can miss one and it's not that big a deal. Well guess what? This is what we do for a living you big goofballs. You've got to make sure that attitude of "I can casually miss a session" is not encouraged in any way. You need to learn to respect your time or clients might run you over.

It is NOT OK for a student to cancel last minute without paying. Last minute cancellations, with almost no exceptions, are PAYMENT DUE in my books. Everything will go over smoothly provided you are clear in your policy that this is not acceptable.

It is NOT OK for a student to ask for a different time after you've been holding a time for them for 3 weeks. If a student wants to switch times, and has a bad habit of switching times, I will say something like "Is there a time each week that you are always free? It's important for me to find a time that is consistent from week to week so that I can plan the rest of my students".

I have built my cancellation policy so that it covers as many of these situations as possible. Here's what I currently use:

Policy Template

Planned Cancellations (cancellations made for the following month)

When you pay for sessions at the start of the month, I ask you to keep to those times. So if there is a sports event or a play or something like that, I ask that you let me know before the start of each month (and before you pay) or sooner, AND at least 2 weeks in advance if you plan to miss a session. Please remember that I reserve your spot and turn other clients away if they ask for it.

Last minute cancellations (made within 24 hours of the session for emergencies)

If you happen to miss or forget a session or have an emergency, I will not ask for payment the first time, but will begin asking for payment the second time and continuing. In other words, clients may, up to once per year, miss a session and not worry about letting me know. I will simply send an email reminding you of the cancellation policy, and we'll move on from there.

Something in between (cancellations made during the month but still in advance)

Let's say you book a session for the end of the month and find out two weeks before that you can't make it. For now, there will be no penalty and I will refund your money or give an alternate time if possible. I'll set the limit at 2 of these per year, and ask for payment of any missed sessions over this limit. Note that any cancellations made 2 weeks before a session or less fall into this category, regardless of if they were made in the preceding month.

This cancellation policy has served me well. I haven't run into any problems thus far when using it. It is also reasonable, given that students' schedules can be rather hectic. You can use a similar policy or tweak it to meet your needs. You could be stricter, but be sure to listen to feedback from clients. If too many are complaining, you may have been a bit unreasonable.

Exceptions

There are also a bunch of exceptions that apply. These are good to include in your policy and clients will appreciate a little extra freedom. Here is my current exceptions policy.

Stat Holidays and other Exceptions

I don't want to work from December 23 until two weeks later on January 6th, so there will be no sessions during that time. I'm such a princess.

1. No one is penalized for missing any stat holidays. A convenient list is found here. Please let me know one way or the other if you will attend, as I will still teach on those days.

2. No one is penalized for missing a session over their school's scheduled March break. I would however expect students to let me know if they plan not to attend, as I still reserve the spot.

3. No one is ever penalized for extreme weather. Stay safe friends! Blizzards, freezing rain etc. are good and fair reasons to stay home. As usual, please let me know either way.

These conditions are subject to change. . Last updated April 30th, 2014

If you create a policy and make it readily available to clients, you're going to avoid a huge potential problem area - dealing with conflict. You'll still have some tricky cases to consider, because there is no policy on earth that covers every possible situation, but a good policy can mitigate many of these situations before they arise.

Remember, if a client is constantly giving you problems and cancelling sessions, they had better be paying for what they miss or you can just cut them loose. The customer is NOT always right. It will hurt your business in the long run to have clients who don't show up on time, who miss sessions and who don't respect your time and constantly ask to switch times. Just cut them out. You'll be freeing up time for a dependable, consistent client.

Client Retention

Let's be honest. You're only as good as the clients you keep. If you can't keep clients past the first session, you're going to be in some big trouble, and you're definitely doing something wrong.

In this chapter we're going to cover everything I've learned about client retention. I've tried a ton of ways to keep my clients coming back, and you'll get the benefit of knowing only the ones that worked. You just got an advantage over the other tutors in your area. Sweet. There are things you'll need to do before, during, and after each session is held.

Before the session

1. Arrive at your location early and make sure it's clean and ready to go. You don't want to be doing any last minute scrambling or seem disorganized.

2. If you are uneasy about material, ask for a sample and prepare before you meet with the

student. It's better to come off a little unsure about the material then to fake it during a session. As we'll see in the next section, faking it is probably the worst thing you can do.

It is completely acceptable to ask for any electronic material before the session. If you are even a little bit unsure of what you'll be teaching, be sure to ask for a copy a few days in advance, if possible.

3. Bring paper, pens, calculator and anything else you might need. It's going to be pretty damn embarrassing if neither of you brought something to write on. They're going to blame you, as they should. Act professional, but be personable as well.

4. Have a system in place to mitigate student cancellations (a clear cancellation policy). Cancellations are killer in this business, and they happen all the time. But you're going to prep for this situation by already having a cancellation policy that the client has read and understood.

During the session

1. Don't talk too much about a topic. The students usually have specific questions that they need

answered, but that doesn't mean that you can just tell them *everything* you know about a subject. It's going to confuse them, and they're going to go home thinking that you're smart, but not an effective tutor.

2. Don't try and answer every single question they have. This might sound backwards but it's true. If they are asking you a question and you think they actually might know the answer, ask them instead.

Student: "Hey Sheldon, if I add ⅖ to ⅗ what do I get?"

I would never answer this question. Instead, I'm going to ask them a series of questions so that *they* can answer it themselves:

First question: "How many fifths are in a whole?
Second question: "If I take 2 of something and 3 of something, how many of that thing do I have?"
Third question: "In this case, I have 2 of what, and I'm adding it to 3 of what?"

Hopefully, the student will then see that they are adding 2 copies of ⅕ and 3 copies of ⅕ for a total of 5 copies of ⅕, which is $^5/_5$ and if you simplify, that's just the number 1 (if math is not your thing then this will make no sense, so don't worry). Use this example as a model of what to do when the student asks questions at their own level.

3. Don't do their work for them. This sounds rather obvious but if you want the student to learn the material, then they have to know how to do the work. Nine times out of ten the student actually wants to learn the material. Oddly enough there are occasions when the student really couldn't give a shit. We'll cover that case in the section about most common mistakes.

4. Don't fake anything. If you don't know, you don't know. This is the single most important rule to follow. If you fake it, they'll know. Typically, when a shit tutor doesn't know what they're talking about, their instinct will be to talk nervously about the subject, or their studying strategies, or their friend who told them about this class, or anything that's *not actually the student's question.* Don't ever do this. If you don't know, and can't figure it out in a minute or two with the help of their notes, tell them "I'm actually not sure, but I'll find out for you". Move on to the next question, but then *follow up with that particular question later,* even via email that night or sometime soon.

After the session

1. Ask for monthly commitments, or even commitments for the term. Don't just say "see ya later!" Instead, ask them if they'd like you to reserve this time as a weekly spot. If they say yes, ask them if they are familiar with the payment policy. Usually, they student or parent will just say "I'm not sure. How should I pay you?" Perfect! Luckily this is how it goes down most of the time. Just reply something like "I ask for monthly payments before the start of the month"

Using a combination of these strategies will go a long way for your client retention. Remember that your tutoring empire is built over time, piece by piece. A success, in terms of business, is a student that had a great experience, came for steady weekly sessions, and then referred you to a friend or teacher any time they could. This is exactly the type of student that you'll be building your empire on, so we need to focus on that type of student. Your effective skills, as opposed to contracts that lock in students for the year, are going to be the key factors in retaining clients. Trying to force long contracts is risky and can reduce your skill level over time (makes you lazy) and you'll get less students and parents having confidence in you.

Quick start guide

OK great, so we've talked about all the theory behind getting clients for an awesome tutoring shop. Now what we need is a one stop shop for how to get up and running right now.

I'm writing this list as though you're starting from scratch. The only thing you're expected to have at this point, is a relatively good mastery over one or more subjects. You should be capable of the 85%-95% grade range of any particular class if you'd like to tutor it. However, exceptions can be made.

Ready to go? Let's do this. This is the 7-day guide on how to get up and running with your new tutoring business in any subject. I'll be referencing the different sections of this book, so if you need more details just go there. I'll assume you have a budget of essentially $0 for marketing. I'll leave out details about how to stay well organized, but that information is in the individual chapters. This is just about how to get students in the door as fast as possible while maintaining good practices.

1. Create a list of 10 high schools in your area using the Zeus Template included in the "The best marketing strategies" section of the book. Get the phone numbers and emails of all the student services offices. Do this for 10 right now, and we'll do the rest later. Send all of them the ad for your tutoring services.

Time frame: One to three hours. Use the Zeus and Challenger Templates for the ad and the tracking of different student services offices.

2. Find at most 3 convenient tutoring spaces around the city. Eventually you'll be using only your best tutoring space and all your clients will come see you there.

Time frame: Take an hour to plan tentative locations. No need to visit them before hand, but as you visit them with students, make notes and be comfortable with changing locations if necessary until you find an awesome one.

3. Post ads on the three most popular free classifieds sites around your location (like Craigslist, Kijiji, etc.). Use the Apollo Template provided. Do the rest later (there are usually around 10 or so such sites)

Time frame: Using the Apollo Template this should only take about 2 hours tops.

4. Add the rest of student services numbers and emails to your list.

Time frame: Do an hour or two of this each night. Don't need to do it all at once

5. Make a list of the high school teachers emails. You might be able to get this information from the school's website but you might have to contact the department head. As you get more emails, start trying to get in touch with teachers and offer your services.

Time frame: Spend an hour or two on this each night as well. Use the Zeus Template to get yourself started.

If you do all these steps and work really hard at them, you'll be up and running in 7 days. It's probably about 20-30 hours of work to get the bare bones work set up. From there, you'll be earning income and can focus on more detailed work like the session tracking and the website.

You just gotta do it. There are no huge shortcuts for this work. So what are you waiting for?

Most common mistakes

Not being personable with your student is going to make them feel uncomfortable. You're not trying to be their best friend, but you need to show that you care. In fact, don't try and be their best friend. That's too close. Make it clear that you're a cool person but that there's nothing that can stop you from getting their grades up.

Your goal is to be somewhere in the "friends" range where they feel comfortable making mistakes around you. Sometimes this is hard to do with students, and they are just so scared and embarrassed to make mistakes. You need to address this right away. See the teaching section for information on how to do this effectively.

Declining students because you're not sure if you know the material well enough. Let me tell you, I wouldn't be where I am today if I only accepted students from classes that I was 100% comfortable with. In fact, I'd say I'm sometimes only 50% confident I'll know the exact answers they seek. I *still* tell the student to come on by, and I ask for some material before the session. 95% of the time the session goes far smoother than I anticipated, and I end up being happy that I took them on. Say yes. Only say no when you *know* that you don't know the class at all.

Not being a leader can mean that your session will get derailed, or that you'll focus on too many things that are not important. You need to make sure that you're working on relevant problems and that the student is working for the full session. For example, if you explained a concept last week and they ask you to re-teach the exact same thing, there might be a motivation issue. Have them work through the problem right in front of you, and have the try and figure it out right then and there. If they aren't doing it at home, then this is the only time they're going to do it.

If they don't persistently fail to respond positively with at least some enthusiasm (even if it's fake), they let out a sigh of frustration because they actually have to do work, or they become annoyed, think about letting that student go. You don't have time to waste your valuable skills on students who are not interested in learning. Trust me, life will be better for both people. Free up that time slot for a student who is more eager to learn.

Taking on students whose main problem is a motivational one is tempting because I think many tutors consider that part of the job. Most kids who don't like math also have a motivational problem towards math, so tutors usually group the two together.

It is not the tutor's job to fix a motivational problem, or to make math fun. That's a tough job and it's not worth our rates. Our job is to break concepts down to reveal the simplicity and beauty of the patterns (which usually is quite fun!). Our job is also to lead the student in a productive, learning intensive session. The student brings the motivation. We bring everything else.

It's a good idea to point out a motivational problem right away. If a student is obviously upset that they are there for tutoring, say something like "You know you don't have to come to tutoring. But if you're going to come, you need to bring your enthusiasm and you really need to want to learn math".

Trying really hard to teach students who don't want to learn is essentially the motivational problem listed above. Don't fight this battle other than a quick "shape up or ship out" comment like above. I wanted to rephrase this problem from a different perspective to give you a higher chance of identifying this particularly problematic circumstance.

Trying to answer nonspecific questions will lead you down a hole with no light at the end. Try going to the doctor and saying "I feel bad" and having him or her guess what to say. Of course, since they are smart, they'll say "where does it hurt?" and then they'll ask about 100 more questions until they know exactly what's wrong. Only then will they begin to offer up solutions.

Our job isn't too much different. If a student comes in with problems in "Chapter 4", then ask them to show you exactly where they are having problems. Address specific questions, not vague feelings of discomfort.

Teaching too many formulas/rules and not enough concepts will make math, science, and language studies a confusing world of hurt for students who are not naturally inclined to absorb such a nerdy collection of otherwise useless information. Although extremely interesting for us nerds, about 90% of the high school curriculum will never be used by most students. Challenge yourself to get a deeper understanding of concepts so you can teach students *why* a formula works and is true, not just *that* the formula works and is true. They'll retain the concepts and perform much better.

Not having a solutions book can be risky. It's much better to be able to check your work even though you are the tutor. You should be getting the answers right anyway, so get used to having solutions books around whenever possible and checking them frequently.

Not having subject mastery will ensure your students go elsewhere very quickly. It's really hard to fake subject mastery. It's better to ask in advance if students can provide you with a list of questions they would like to go over than to be blindsided at the session and not be able to help out at all.

Every time a student asks you a question that you are unfamiliar with, follow up with them and learn the topic.

FAQ

Will a young student (16 or under) really be comfortable coming over to my apartment?

If you have been referred to the parent of the student by another client, and especially a teacher, then yes. About 5% of my clients indicate they are uncomfortable having their child come to my house. The other 95% are fine with it. Sometimes the parents come with the students for the first session and that's about it.

How do I start tutoring if I don't have testimonials or references?

Testimonials are nothing compared to a referral. Testimonials are not what they are cracked up to be. Don't worry about them. In terms of references, I have only been asked for references about 3 times in 15 years of tutoring.

How often can I miss a session?

You should follow your own cancellation policy as

well. If you want to miss a session or take a week off or something, let the client know well in advance. Try to NEVER cancel a session at the last minute. Set a standard for yourself and keep to it.

Do I need to follow up after each session and see how it went?

No, this is your job. You should act as though you are a great tutor, and a great tutor wouldn't call after a session to check if he is still a great tutor. If however, there is something concerning about the student, it's a great idea to let the parents know! Same thing goes if you notice something awesome about the student or if the student is working extra hard.

How do I know I'm ready to tutor?

Do you love your subject? Are you pretty damn good at it? Do you love teaching others the stuff you know? Does it make you feel pretty good? Do you like it when someone else is thankful that you could help them learn? If you said yes to most of those, then you're probably a good fit to be a tutor.

How much money should I expect to be making and how soon should I expect to be making it?

If you follow the guidelines in this text and work about 5 hours a day on the business and marketing, I would expect to get clients within a month to be able to make $500-$800, depending on your skill level. After 6 months you should be extremely comfortable financially making about 1.5-3k per month.

What happens if a student really doesn't want to learn?

When you run into these students, and you will, it's pretty much the worst case scenario. They don't want to be there, and it makes the session feel like it's taking forever. Not only that, but the student is barely progressing so the parents are wasting their money. Nobody wins. If you run into these students, just politely tell their parents that it isn't working out, and that you need their child to be more motivated for sessions. It doesn't matter if they are a slow student or way behind - it just matters that *they want to learn,* and you can't teach that.

Do you ever offer makeup sessions if you couldn't answer all their questions?

No, I have never ever done a makeup session. It's just not something that the client ever expects. They'll leave you and go to another tutor before they ask for a make up session.

What do I do when the student frequently replies with "that's what I said" when you correct them?

Occasionally you run into a know-it-all. It's frustrating, especially if you are a bit cocky like me :P Some possible responses are:

"Ah, then I must have heard you wrong. Don't shoot!"
"Well, now you know it twice as well!"
"Oh good, I was just testing you."
"Oh cool, then you can tutor me instead!"

Just brush it off. If they get really frustrating you can stop teaching and start asking questions about the material for them to explain to you. That way they'll be doing all the talking and won't really be able to tell you "that's what I said" or something slightly bratty like that.

FAREWELL

It's taken me about 10 years to come up with a smooth tutoring shop. Everything from the marketing to the actual teaching now runs very nicely, and it's allowed me to live a ridiculously hassle free life. I never worry about money. I work about 15 hours a week and earn about 5k per month, which covers all my expenses very easily.

I want to make one thing clear for you, the reader, before you embark on this journey. No matter what, you're going to need to have some grit. In other words, you're going to need to overcome challenges. If you're not prepared to do that, then you're not going to be able to make it in this industry, or any other industry.

The other quality that you're going to need is versatility.

When you encounter a roadblock, don't just try and plow through it if you can just walk around.

Grit + Versatility = Winning

If you get used to dealing with challenges and being versatile, nothing will stop you and you'll be well on your way to becoming a successful tutor. Remember that someone who is not a smart as you has probably gotten a tutoring business up and running before, so why can't you? You have everything you need.

Best of luck. Now can you do me one huge favour? It's really important to me that you go and earn some money now. I want you working hard and using what you've learned in this book right now. Nothing would make me happier than to know I'm helping you make your financial situation awesomely successful. If this book has been helpful to you please email me (tallguytutoring@gmail.com) and let me know. I would be extremely happy and grateful to hear from you all.

Success

Success

what people think
it looks like

what it really
looks like